Friendship is the only cement that will ever hold the world together.
– *Woodrow T. Wilson*

Contents

Poetry

From The Manse Window

iStock.

Nature's Calendar

Illustrations by Sarah Holliday and Mandy Dixon.

Welcome To Spring!

THOUGH winter's grip was everywhere,
A subtle change is in the air:
We leave behind the ice and snow
As now, more gentle breezes blow.

Here, bursting forth from frozen ground,
New signs of life are to be found:
The pale green spears of life anew
As snowdrops manage to break through.

And as we look around we find
The daffodils not far behind:
Their yellow heads sway in the breeze
And buds show green on hawthorn trees.

The dandelions chase the sun,
Then close before the day is done
To open as a ball of white
From which a host of seeds takes flight.

Where formerly the trees were bare,
Now busy birds are nesting there.
Dawn choruses to greet each day
And wildlife's never far away.

In spring we see a wondrous show
As meadow flowers start to grow,
And hawthorn trees are clad in May –
With summer days not far away.

Dennis W. Turner.

7

Butterflies

THE garden, chilled by winter's cold,
Looks drab until a flash of gold,
A flutter of a coloured wing,
Shows promise of the coming spring.

No better sight to please the eyes,
And lift the heart, than butterflies!
Their joyful flight such hope conveys
Of bluer skies and warmer days.

Small tortoiseshells and brimstones, too,
Alight on blossoms born anew;
The orange-tip and cabbage white
Flit high and low in sheer delight.

Bright butterflies, I hope you stay,
And fill my garden every day,
To linger through the sunny hours
And dance among the springtime flowers.

Maggie Ingall.

The Girl In The Photo

WHO is the girl in the black and white photo,
Curly fair hair and a freckly nose?
We hadn't yet met when this picture was taken,
So little we knew of how quickly time goes.

Who is the girl in the white velvet jacket,
Posing with flowers, and me by her side?
That was the day we put rings on our fingers;
The happiest man with that girl as his bride.

Who is the girl with the family of children,
Playing on beaches, in parks or by streams?
A proud, loving father was taking the photos,
Sharing the sunshine, the fun and the dreams.

And now who's the girl in the ruby-red ballgown,
Holding me close as I whirl her around?
Forty years married, a lifetime to treasure,
We open the album and memories abound.

Carla Burns.

A Country Lane

TO wander down a country lane
On a day in early spring,
We notice all the lovely things,
The changing seasons bring.

The tiny buds upon the trees,
In varied shades of green;
Pale primroses on woodland edge,
Where windflowers, too, are seen.

The celandines whose golden glow
Is like a ray of sun,
Which shows that winter's reign is past
And springtime has begun.

To listen to the song of birds
As nesting time draws near,
And watch, as daylight hours increase,
For swallows to appear.

To do these things will bring us joy
And lift our hearts anew.
They prove that springtime has begun
And winter's reign is through.

Rosemary Bennett.

March

AT times March is a tug-of-war
With winter versus spring –
Where winter tries to hold its ground
By trying hard to bring
Cold icy winds and even snow,
But we can feel the sun.
And though we may not feel our toes
We hope that spring has won!

The snowdrop is the first to peep
Its head above the ground;
Then daffodils and crocuses
Soon spring up all around.
The trees then show a haze of green
And how the birds now sing!
And when that first new lamb appears
We know – yes! This is spring!

Eileen Hay.

from the Manse Window

The Hand Of Friendship

CHRISTMAS DAY was quite memorable a few years ago. I was kept a prisoner in my own home!

Before you call the police, I should explain.

I was confined to an armchair in the corner of the room, after being knocked down in an accident one morning. I was not able to get up and help at all. In fact, it was quite humbling to have to ask my family for help if I wanted to go to the bathroom.

Many times we are encouraged to help others, but it is just as important to be able to receive help – otherwise the helpers would have no-one to help. If we took a moment to think about it, most of us would agree that without the love and care from others around us, things would be very different.

Unfortunately, the way I came to appreciate this was rather dramatic.

I was walking to work, when suddenly a car came out of nowhere (or so it seemed) and knocked me to the ground. Quite a few people came out of the church nearby and asked what they could do. I was unsure how to respond to the help offered – and I have since found out that is a common reaction, as we struggle to come to terms with what has happened.

I was convinced I could just get up and continue on my journey, and it took a few minutes to realise I couldn't move my legs, so walking was out of the question.

It sometimes takes quite a traumatic thing to happen to you to make you realise who your friends are.

Of course, one advantage of belonging to a church community is having a ready-made group of friends, so it's sad that I only came to appreciate them when so many people made the effort to help me while I was in hospital. In fact, I think I can confidently say that those friends made a huge difference to my life, as I took the time to rest and feel loved and cared for.

Even the nurses commented on how many visitors I had and how many cards I received.

When I was moved to a

▶

iStock.

By Kathrine Davey, Methodist Preacher.

▶ private room, I was able to talk to various visitors in confidence, and we had several long conversations. I knew many people who worked in the hospital, as it is not unusual for a lot of churches to have a good representation from the caring professions. I'd like to think that they are attracted because of the caring nature of the church. Unfortunately, that's not always the case.

Perhaps that's because the church is made up of people with human foibles, and not plaster saints, which don't contribute much to the world.

When I first arrived in hospital, there was some concern that I was not breathing independently, so I was sent to the critical care ward. An oxygen mask covered most of my face; this had to be worn day and night and prevented me from speaking. My breathing was monitored regularly and improvement was slow.

However, even then, my recovery was down to the arrival of friends. A family member was brought by a friend and I was so determined to be able to hold a conversation with them that the nurses let me use a temporary mask that didn't muffle my speech. From that moment on we all realised that I was able to manage with just that mask and I didn't have to go back to the one which made me seem so much more helpless.

In just a few days, I was able to go down to the ordinary ward, where my stream of visitors increased quickly, especially as word spread among the church family that I was in hospital. I was able to use the telephone to keep informed of events – so much so that I sometimes knew more about local happenings than my visitors!

The nurse there had the usual brief questionnaire to fill in. He read out the questions and when he asked, "Do you want to see a chaplain?", I replied, "You're too late. I've already seen four!"

In fact, one of the chaplains commented on the fact that it was the first time he had been offered a cup of tea by the ward staff. Perhaps they realised that we would both have a lot to talk about.

Finally I was allowed home. Well, not quite home, because I went to stay with my mother in her bungalow until I could cope with climbing stairs. Even then my recovery was dependent on others, and my first faltering steps were due to a friend's intervention.

My mum was out when the telephone rang, so I leaned over to try to answer it. It was just that little bit too far out of reach, yet I was so determined to be able to say that I had reached the telephone in time, that I pulled myself along with the help of the chairs and the sofa, just like children do when they are learning to walk.

Fortunately, I got to the phone in time and heard a familiar voice. One of our church leaders wanted to come and visit me.

That moment was the beginning of the realisation that I was recovering and returning to the health that I had enjoyed before my accident.

So, despite the many books I had read over the years, I came to appreciate the value of others, and their friendship, through an experience gained in the most trying of circumstances.

When I was first carried into the ambulance, one of the paramedics asked bitterly, "Well, where was God a few minutes ago when you needed him?"

I didn't reply at the time, but my answer could well have been, "I don't know, but I do know that this accident helped me to learn the value of friendship." ■

Nature's Calendar For *Spring*

Lenticular clouds form at high altitudes. More commonly found in mountainous regions, they are often formed by the high peaks (or at least the wind streams they generate). They can often be seen up to 60 miles away from the mountain that may have caused their formation.

Polar bears are the only bears that don't hibernate, given that winter is the climate they're designed for! Did you know a polar bear can swim up to 100 miles at a time? Hence their Latin name *Ursus maritimus* meaning "sea bear".

Rafflesia Arnoldii are mostly found in the forests of Sumatra and are the biggest individual flowers in the world, growing up to three feet across. They don't smell too good, though, so keep your distance!

Vietnam has been becoming more and more accessible to tourists for a while, and now's the perfect chance to explore its blend of history and stunning scenery. March is a great time of year to visit, as the humidity eases up and the country has its driest month.

Watercress is starting to come into season in the UK, and its return to fame over recent years is thanks in no small part to its huge nutritional content. It contains more Vitamin C than oranges and more calcium than milk!

The Iranian New Year, Nowruz, begins on the vernal equinox – the first day of spring. It's the first day of the first month of the Iranian calendar, and since the collapse of the Soviet Union has spread to other countries in Asia.

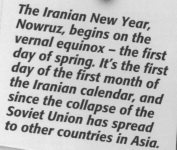

21

Help Wanted!

WHAT is it I'm doing wrong
When it comes to opening things?
Some bottle tops are challenging.
Oh, and tins of beans with rings.

Pull the ring to open can.
Sauce flies out – I'm mottled.
Grip top firmly, squeeze and turn.
I hate those caps on bottles.

Tops with little collars say
Pull tag and peel around.
Without good sight and fingernails,
Not as easy as it sounds.

Sometimes we're told, *To open lid
Press firmly down, then twist*.
That's all right if you possess
A strong and healthy wrist.

I battle with the wrapping
On biscuits, chocolate, cakes.
Hard plastic casing sealed on card
Is very hard to break.

Do you have such trouble,
Or is it only me?
Thank heavens I'm still able
To open a box of tea!

Thelma Moss.

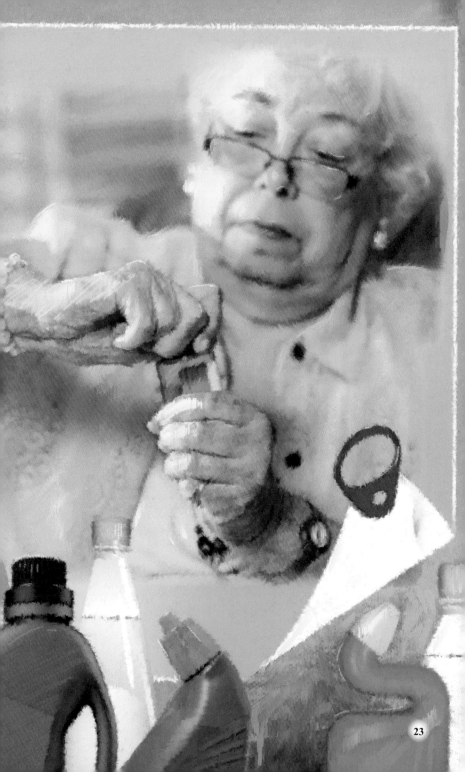

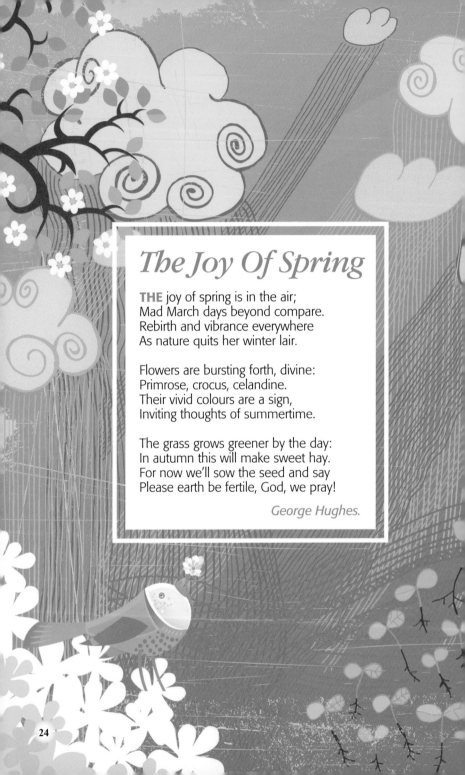

The Joy Of Spring

THE joy of spring is in the air;
Mad March days beyond compare.
Rebirth and vibrance everywhere
As nature quits her winter lair.

Flowers are bursting forth, divine:
Primrose, crocus, celandine.
Their vivid colours are a sign,
Inviting thoughts of summertime.

The grass grows greener by the day:
In autumn this will make sweet hay.
For now we'll sow the seed and say
Please earth be fertile, God, we pray!

George Hughes.

Three Hills

BETWEEN Somerset and Dorset,
Three faerie hills are found;
And if you stray there unaware,
You'll be on hallowed ground.

Dancing Hill – a windy hill –
Resounds with breezy laughter,
But stops short at the end of town,
And loses voice soon after.

Zig-zag Hill winds round and round,
Surprises on each bend;
Uncertain of the path to take,
It seems to have no end.

But birdsong greets the passer-by,
Who walks up Cuckoo Hill;
And though the seasons come and go,
A cuckoo sings there still.

Dawn Lawrence.

Spring's Full Glory

TIME of change and of beginning;
Time of earlier morning light.
Last snow melting, last frost thinning –
Green reborn from winter white,
This is spring, at last it's here!
This is the dawning of the year.

Days grow milder, brighter, longer;
Buds poke through, daring and shy.
Sunlight gradually grows stronger,
As it casts its golden eye
On the world where all awakes,
Nature making no mistakes.

But there still are strong winds gusting,
Still are squally showers that fall,
And we must endure them, trusting
That the springtime needs them all
To blow away the winter air,
And nurture newborn nature there.

Now it's May, and spring's full glory
Blossoms forth on fields and trees.
Soft bright colours tell a story
Full of dreams and memories,
And on many a village green
An ancient dance can still be seen.

Deborah Mercer.

New Life

WHEN winter holds us in its grasp
Spring seems so far away –
We feel that it will never come
Then all at once, one day
We spy a snowdrop peeping through
The cold, hard winter ground,
And suddenly we dare to hope
The seasons have turned round!

The wind can hold a biting edge
As chilly winter lingers,
But eager gardeners can feel
A tingling in green fingers!
And then it seems that life bursts forth
As springtime bulbs are seen,
And winter-fusty houses need
A really good spring clean!

With newborn lambs and Easter chicks
New life is everywhere,
And winter gloom is banished with
The warmth of mellow air.
If inward-looking winter is
A time of calm reflection,
Then graveyards filled with daffodils
Show joyous resurrection.

Eileen Hay.

The Month Of May

THE month when spring has really sprung,
When nature's at her best,
When gardens, woods and countryside,
With lovely flowers are blessed.

When busy birds are feeding young,
But still find time to sing,
And brightly coloured butterflies
Once more are on the wing.

When woods are dressed in shades of green,
Above a bluebell sea,
And purple foxgloves, standing tall,
Attract the passing bee.

With all these lovely things around,
In verdant bright array,
We greet once more with great delight
The merry month of May.

Rosemary Bennett.

A Closer Look

I SAW a lovely view last week:
I snapped it straightaway;
And with that done, I went to leave,
But something made me stay.
I paused to look more closely still,
And found myself amazed
At all the things I'd nearly missed
When first I stopped and gazed.

The subtle shades of distant hills,
The greens, the blues, the golds,
The shadow of the puffy clouds
That drifted o'er the wolds.
A river winding far away,
A boat, bound who-knows-where,
The joyful song of airborne lark,
The scent of sun-warmed air.

Next time, though I may take a snap,
I'll also make quite sure
To capture how it really feels,
To keep for evermore.

Maggie Ingall.

The Light Of The World

ONE of the joys of spring is when the evenings begin slowly to get lighter, bit by bit, day after day. It lifts the spirits to imagine the long summer days ahead after a dark and dreary winter. Even when it rains it doesn't seem to matter quite so much when it's light.

Some people who suffer from SAD find that winter is particularly hard for them. As I get older the gloom gets me down more than it did in my younger days. To see the first snowdrops in the park, the early crocuses and daffodils, and to hear the ethereal song of a blackbird in the dusk brings tears of joy to my eyes.

We are people of light, and we need the light. When Terry Waite was held hostage in Beirut all those years ago, he was deprived of light, blindfolded and locked in a cell with no access to daylight. It's a miracle that he didn't go mad.

When he was eventually released, it took a while to adjust to the brilliance of sunlight. It's no mistake that dungeons have always been in the deepest, darkest parts of castles. Depriving prisoners of light is all part of trying to break the spirit.

Many years ago when I was a student, I had just climbed into the tiny lift in the halls of residence when there was a power cut. I was trapped between floors and the only thing that stopped me from panicking was the fact that there was a small glass panel in the lift door through which filtered a measure of daylight. I was relieved when the power was restored within 10 minutes!

The book of Genesis tells us that when the world was created, God said, "Let there be light!" and there was, and it was good. Like us, waiting for the lighter days of spring, the Creation waited for light, and when it happened it must have been spectacular.

When the Apollo 8 astronauts came around the dark side of the moon, they saw the Earth rise – the first humans ever to witness such a thing – and they quoted the opening verses of Genesis.

Our planet looked like a glorious blue jewel in the darkness of space, glowing as it reflected the light of the sun. It's an iconic image, a

iStock.

by Rev. Susan Sarapuk.

▶ stark reminder of how essential light is.

Then the world was waiting for Jesus. At the beginning of his gospel, John says of Jesus, "In him was life and that life was the light of men. The light shines in the darkness and the darkness has not overcome it." (John 1:4-5)

It is so obvious that, left to our own devices, no matter how good we try to be, we are basically selfish. And when we act selfishly darkness prevails.

Jesus began to change that. People were amazed at his teaching because he had authority and he was so different from the hypocrisy of their religious leaders. He wasn't harsh, critical, judgemental, morose, or bound up in human rules and regulations. Here was someone who knew God intimately and lived in freedom and joy. No wonder crowds followed him – it really was like light coming into dark places, as if the long winter of bondage had ended.

When Jesus calls us to follow him, as his disciples we no longer walk in darkness. We suddenly see the way things are and our place in the universe. We're not in full daylight yet because the kingdom is not here in all its fullness, so we're still affected by darkness. But we have the Light of the World to navigate us through difficult and trying times.

Think of Martha and Mary in deep grief over the death of their brother. They'd been full of hope that Jesus would come and heal him, yet he hadn't and Lazarus had died. Despite this they still had hope. When Jesus told Martha that her brother would rise again, she said, "I know he will rise again in the resurrection at the last day." (John 11.24)

She wasn't in despair about what would ultimately happen. She knew there

was light in the darkness even though there wasn't any in that moment. She made a statement of faith. And we know what happened next – Jesus said that he was the resurrection and the life and went on to raise Lazarus back to life. That was a day of light!

We still go through our dark times. Grief cannot be brushed aside when we are bereaved, and anxiety still gnaws at us when bad things happen or problems arise in our lives. But we are not living in winter. We know that it is getting lighter. Faith holds on to this belief even when nothing seems to be happening to make things better, so the darkness doesn't overwhelm us.

"Now faith is being sure of what we hope for and certain of what we do not see." (Hebrews 11:1.)

But sometimes we do get glimpses. When Peter, James and John went up the mountain with Jesus and saw him with Moses and Elijah it was as if a door to the real world had opened. Jesus shone with such a bright light that it was almost indescribable and rendered them – well, not exactly speechless – overcome with awe, maybe. They had been privileged to get a glimpse of reality.

And so are we when we trust the one who is the light of the world. He reassures us that winter is over, and that sin and death and darkness are dealt with. It is spring – it's getting lighter and we're on our way to summer. And as part of that he calls us to be carriers of the light, to let people know that spring is here and there is no longer any need to dwell in the darkness of winter. Why wouldn't we want to share such good news with everyone? ■

Nature's Calendar For *Spring*

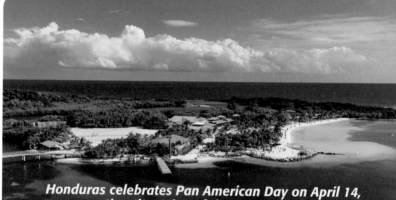

Honduras celebrates Pan American Day on April 14, commemorating the union of the American countries. The Pan American Highway connects North America with South America by road, except for 100 miles at the Darien Gap, a stretch of rainforest on the border of Colombia and Panama.

Crab season begins around April, and whether you're just planning on having some fun with the family, capturing them and plopping them back in, or actually eating them, you'll see more of them now the winter's over. Crab is a great source of protein, without the saturated fat of other meats.

iStock.

The city that straddles the divide between East and West, Istanbul is a bustling place that's easy to get to from almost anywhere. May's a good time to visit, before the sun is too hot. Explore the bazaars and art galleries to the beautiful sound of the mosques' calls to prayer.

Mimosa pudica is known as the shy plant in South America. It has a primitive nervous system that responds to touch – its leaves fold up immediately.

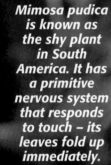

Chipmunks become fully active again through April and May, after a period of winter hibernation. They're still periodically active during the winter, but when they fall asleep their heart rates drop from as much as 350 bpm to as low as 4!

Crepuscular rays are the official title of rays of sun breaking through clouds. They're common around sunrise and sunset. The Ancient Greeks believed it was so the sun could draw water from the earth.

41

A Spider's Eye View

I MAY just be a spider,
But my life is precious, too,
And I don't want to find myself
Trapped underneath your shoe.

I am such a simple soul,
Just waiting for a fly,
Contented to anticipate
One will come zooming by.

I'll wrap it in a parcel,
So neat and deftly done,
For, to chaps like little me,
It's all part of the fun!

I'll store it in the pantry,
In "Best before" date order.
Our dining-room will no doubt be
Down by the flower border.

So, if we can call a special truce,
Our lives would be just fine.
If you could just go your way,
And I will just go mine!

Brian H. Gent.

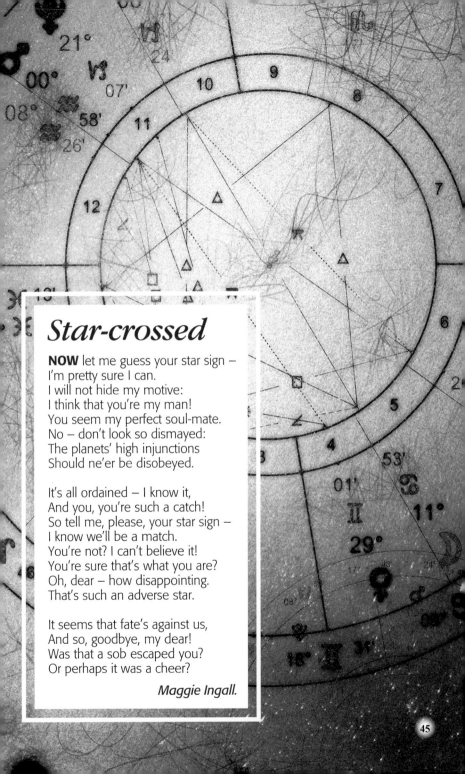

Star-crossed

NOW let me guess your star sign –
I'm pretty sure I can.
I will not hide my motive:
I think that you're my man!
You seem my perfect soul-mate.
No – don't look so dismayed:
The planets' high injunctions
Should ne'er be disobeyed.

It's all ordained – I know it,
And you, you're such a catch!
So tell me, please, your star sign –
I know we'll be a match.
You're not? I can't believe it!
You're sure that's what you are?
Oh, dear – how disappointing.
That's such an adverse star.

It seems that fate's against us,
And so, goodbye, my dear!
Was that a sob escaped you?
Or perhaps it was a cheer?

Maggie Ingall.

The May Tree

THE hawthorn is the may tree –
Its leaves were carved in wood
In churches and cathedrals
For longevity and good.
Once known as the fairies' tree,
Its blossom and its berries
Were used for remedies and cures,
Fruity wine and jellies.

The lover's tree, in poetry,
It crowned the Queen of May;
With boughs around the Maypole
That made a rich display.
And though bad luck might follow
Should the blossom come indoors,
The protective hedge it offered
Spoke highly for its cause.

Its young leaves once provided food
For children who had none –
"Bread and Cheese", the hawthorn
Was known to everyone.
And may, that grows with oak and ash,
Is thorn, the hawthorn tree;
A tree still wild, enchanted,
That grows for you and me.

Dawn Lawrence.

In The Summertime

GOLDEN days that seem unending;
Heady perfume fills the air;
Heavy velvet roses bending,
Leaving silent sweetness there.
Languid light around us glows,
Kissing every fragrant rose.

When the heat of day is strongest,
When we need to seek some shade,
When the days are at their longest,
We can find a woodland glade;
See the light and hazy heat
Dapple down, dance at our feet.

Butterflies flutter and hover,
Like winged rainbows all day long.
From dawn to dusk, swift songbirds cover
Miles with their full-throated song.
All seem to revel and to thrive,
Joyful just to be alive.

Golden sands with children playing,
Hunting memories cloaked in shells.
What is the grand old ocean saying
As it ebbs and flows and swells?
There's something glorious and free
And mighty in the sun-kissed sea.

Summer days that seem unending,
But the sun will set at last.
Rays like rivers, glowing, bending,
Over hills and water cast
Jewelled sunsets, then, next morn,
Another golden day is born!

Deborah Mercer.

The Storm

I ALWAYS knew when it was going to thunder;
The hot day held its breath,
The edges of the sky turned orange,
Like the colour I remembered from a fever.

I had known windless days before,
But this was different; held breath
That you could hear. Birds swam the sky
As though escaping something that wasn't there.

I watched the window; waited
As bits of thunder muttered up above,
Like the grandfather I had never known –
Tramping in an attic for a missing shoe.

A squirm of lightning. Silence:
I listened for the seconds – one, two, three, four –
Until the answering growl of anger came,
The hissing of hot raindrops on the leaves.

I didn't know what it was I wanted,
But it thudded in me like a drum;
I felt a boy from once upon a time
Who longed for fires and dance and magic.

Kenneth Steven.

51

The Safari Park

WE'RE going on safari!
A coach trip to the park,
A stately home attraction –
We're sure to have a lark!

The journey's quite a long one –
We stop awhile en route.
It's time to take refreshments,
Then off again – toot, toot!

The coach is rather stuffy;
We're full of tea and cake.
We reach the lion enclosure –
But no-one is awake!

The tigers roar and rumble;
Hyenas strut and scream;
The monkeys jeer and gibber –
But us? We doze and dream.

I'm sure it was amazing –
At least, that's what they say . . .
Perhaps we'll get together
And try another day!

Maggie Ingall.

Times To Remember

YOUTH – where time did not exist.
Just sun-filled hours to stretch away
By curving brook, where willows trailed
Their lacy fronds at water's edge.
Reeds grew tall, to cast a shade,
And cooling breeze reduced the heat;
The fragrance of the summer air,
Brought dreams of some now distant
　　place.
That charming scene – a view to frame,
To etch for ever on the mind;
To reminisce on passing years,
To let us know – time really flies!

Elizabeth Gozney.

Song Of Summer

COME sing a song of summer,
Come sing along, and dance.
It's time to lift dull spirits,
And if I had the chance,
I'd soar among the swallows,
I'd buzz among the bees,
On thistledown I'd travel,
Afloat upon a breeze.
I'd pick a poppy's petals
To be my summer clothes,
And when I tired of dancing,
I'd sleep within a rose.
Sweet summer, won't you linger?
Please stay, please stay awhile,
For when the sun is shining
The whole world seems to smile.

Maggie Ingall.

from the Manse Window

A View From Above

IN the range of sand dunes near my parental home there is one sand hill that is known, somewhat poetically, as Bird Mountain.

On a clear day, from its relatively modest height, it really does seem as if you can see for ever.

To the south, the mountains of Snowdonia emerge hazily from the mist across the Mersey and Dee estuaries, and gradually give way to the angular towers and blocks of the Liverpool skyline. The horizon softens again as buildings melt into greenly undulating countryside, gently rising towards Aughton-on-the-Hill, its church tower thrusting into the sky like a land-locked lighthouse.

Beyond Aughton the country becomes bleaker and higher; the vast bulk of Winter Hill rises starkly against the sky, radio masts peppering its summit.

The unmistakeable mass of Pendle Hill looms broodingly over the Lancashire plain and, beyond, the stony spine that forms the Pennine chain weaves its way northwards into the far distance. Moving westwards, we are back at the coast again, with Blackpool's famous tower appearing to nestle at the foot of the mountains of the southern Lake District.

Past the tower lies the Irish Sea, inviting the observer to reflect on the mysteries hidden within its inky depths and the tantalising possibilities beyond its horizon.

All this beauty, from a height of no more than 20 or 30 feet!

High places of all kinds may capture our imagination quite powerfully. One of my very earliest memories is of being taken by my parents to visit an uncle in Scotland when I was two years old.

We were living with my grandparents in Liverpool at that time; it was a very urban environment and this visit marked my first encounter with the splendour of the Scottish mountains.

Young as I was, I can vividly remember standing on the pavement outside my uncle's house, staring awestruck at the vision of grandeur on the horizon.

Looking back through the years with my child's mind's-eye, the mountains are colossal and ▶

iStock.

By Rev. Barbara Mosse.

▶ snow-capped, their outlines etched crisply against a sky of vivid blue. I couldn't verbally express what I felt then, but a powerful sense of the beauty and mystery of those majestic and brooding heights has remained with me to this day.

That memory lingered at the back of my mind when, many years later, I accompanied a group of excited ten-year-olds up Helvellyn in the Lake District with a number of other school staff. I'd been looking forward to the trip for months! I'd seen photographs of some of the staggering views visible from the top of the mountain, and couldn't wait to see them for myself.

I was familiar with some of the Lake District countryside, chiefly from my experiences of the two flooded-out Girl Guides camps I had endured there in my teenage years.

Despite the inclement weather on those occasions, I had developed a keen love of the area, though only from ground and lake level. This outing was to be my first venture into the mountains.

We prepared the children well: no-one was allowed to go without strong walking boots, suitably warm and waterproof clothing, bottled water and basic food supplies. We set off from the foot of the mountain in good spirits and fine weather.

Those of you who are familiar with the Lake District won't be surprised to hear that the inevitable happened. No, not drenching rain on this occasion, but just short of the summit and with frightening speed, we found ourselves enveloped in a swirling, impenetrable mountain mist, shutting us off abruptly from all viewpoints and reducing our visibility to a few yards.

Fortunately we were able to wait safely in some of the circular stone roofless structures built on the mountainside for the safety and protection of the sheep. The biblical image of Jesus as the Good Shepherd came to mind.

Thankfully, an hour or so later the mist lifted, and we were able to make our way down the mountain safely.

Mountains and hills can make for powerful experiences of wonder, awe and sometimes fear and danger. They appear regularly in the bible, often with great significance.

In the Old Testament, Moses met God on Mount Sinai in cloud and fire and thunder just before the giving of the Ten Commandments. In contrast, the prophet Elijah encountered God on Mount Horeb in "a still, small voice", or as one of the modern translations puts it: "a sound of sheer silence".

The writer of Psalm 121 instinctively lifts his eyes to the hills when seeking divine help and inspiration. And some of the New Testament's most significant events also occurred on mountains.

Jesus's transfiguration took place on a mountain in the company of his three closest disciples, as did the body of his teaching now famously known as the Sermon on the Mount. At times Jesus would withdraw completely from both

the crowds and his disciples to pray alone on a mountain.

There may be any number of reasons why we may not be able to get out into the countryside and do our own climbing. But we shouldn't lose heart because all of us can certainly appreciate our hill and mountain landscape from ground level.

Even if we are not able to get out into the countryside and see the real thing, a few minutes sitting quietly with a photo or painting, or a nature programme on the television, can help disperse the shadows which so easily cloud our mind and spirit.

There is a beautiful thanksgiving prayer from the Celtic tradition which ends with these words: "And as the mist scatters on the crest of the hills, may each ill haze clear from my soul, O God."

As I stood on Bird Mountain, buffeted by the bracing wind which continually blows in off the Irish Sea, my anxieties and concerns were gradually shrinking and I began to see things with a greater sense of proportion.

When I at last descended to ground level, my heart felt lighter; I was breathing more easily, and ready to face the challenges of the day with renewed heart. ■

Nature's Calendar For *Summer*

In the northern hemisphere, June is a great time to explore places that experience long winters. Visit Copenhagen and enjoy the traditional theme park at Tivoli Gardens or head out of town to one of the world-class art galleries.

Coleus was brought back from Indonesia to the UK in the mid-19th century, and despite being dismissed by some as just a "fashionable weed", it is still popular with gardeners. However, they are hard to sustain in Britain as they need a good year-round temperature – they should only be planted out when it reaches 21 deg. C.

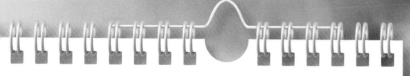

The box turtle sleeps for around 150 days of the year, only putting in an appearance for the good weather. They live in the US and Mexico, and are unique in that their lower shell is hinged, allowing them to withdraw into it almost completely – helping contribute to their long lifespan of about 100 years.

Back in 1976, June marked the start of a record heatwave in the UK. Temperatures stayed at 30 deg. C. or more for 15 consecutive days at Heathrow, and it followed on from a dry winter. Some parts of the south-west didn't see rain for over 45 days during the summer.

Green beans have been cultivated by people for around 7,000 years, and require good weather to be at their best – above 20 deg. C. Selling around 15 million tons per year, China is by far the largest exporter of beans.

On June 28, Taiwan celebrates the birthday of Kuan Kung, the god of war. His birthday is celebrated because he protects good folk from anyone who wishes them harm or wants to take advantage of them. He's also a god of wealth, bringing prosperity to any house that has an image of him in it.

A Click In Time

I'VE just acquired a camera
In bright kingfisher blue.
A magic "Open Sesame!"
To take great vistas new.

I must be at the ready
To snap the sea's repose,
And up there in a fresco sky
The sunset's fiery close.

Cirrus clouds in the bluest blue
And a quaint old harbour scene,
A sandy beach, and pearl shells
And rock pools, shining green.

Then I'll do a photo shoot
Of craggy mountains low:
The moors, the gorse and heather,
Curlew's sweep, and streams in flow.

So with my trusty camera
A wonderful world, I see,
My store of scenes to treasure
And all is heavenly.

Dorothy McGregor.

A Moorland Meditation

WALK with me on a heather moor –
The peace is ours to share.
We'll pause to hear the wild birds call,
With time to stand and stare.
The moorland path goes on and on,
The world seems far away –
The quiet touches heart and soul
On this delightful day.

The scene of wood-smoke drifts around
From gardens far below,
And fleecy clouds go floating by
As gentle breezes blow.
Walk with me on a heather moor
And leave all care behind.
Just close your eyes and we'll be there,
In spirit, heart and mind.

Iris Hesselden.

The Island Of Coll

I GOT up long before the dawn;
Opened an unlocked door
Into a landscape of moor and loch,
Twelve years old: the only danger
  barbed-wire fences.
I ran until the hillside turned to sand,
And under me the whole Atlantic
Softening the white rim of the island
Like a sigh. I chased down all the dunes,
Barefooting sand so white it might have
  been
A kind of snow. Sea breathed
In ledges and descents, in many blues
That melted into one. I dared undress
To tread out deep until I lifted
Held and unafraid, breath
Caught and stolen by the cold,
I entered another world;
Melted into something else,
I came out strange and shining, new
And wandered slowly home, the same –
Yet never quite the same again.

Kenneth Steven.

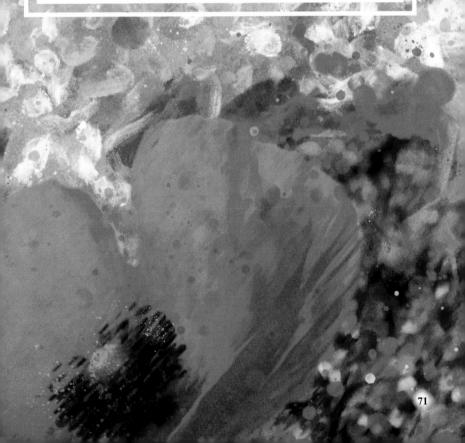

The Bumblebee

A LITTLE bumblebee I am, all furry, yellow, black.
My two hind legs hold pockets for the pollen that I pack.
I bumble and I rumble, whenever I'm around;
It's something that I'm famous for, my lovely buzzing sound.

And I do something no-one else but bumblebees can do;
It's called buzz pollination – something strange but nothing new.
I grab a flower and give a buzz of very high-pitched tone,
And that releases pollen – an act for which I'm known.

But don't confuse me with the wasp, or honeybees that sting;
You can hold me on your finger and watch me rest and cling.
And don't think it's just showy blooms that pass the nectar test –
It's mostly wild plants, pollen rich, that all we bees love best!

Dawn Lawrence.

Little Teashop

I LOVE a little teashop when the days are dark and drear;
The mist rolls through the valleys and nothing's bright or clear.
Its lights shine out in promise of a cosy world within –
While the doorbell chimes a welcome to all who enter in.

The gentle clink of teacups is really all it takes,
With silver stands o'erflowing with sandwiches and cakes,
Amidst the hum of chatter as friends catch up on news –
Forget the fancy restaurants, there is nothing else I'd choose.

Yes, I love a little teashop when the rain is pelting down
And bright umbrellas mushroom as folk scurry through the town.
It's the perfect place to linger and enjoy an hour or two
And complain about the weather till the skies once more turn blue.

But in the summer sunshine, on long, lazy afternoons,
When tea is served alfresco with cream scones and macaroons,
I'd live it to the last crumb, from the teapots to the sign,
Perhaps you think I'm biased but, you see, the teashop's mine!

Marian Cleworth.

End Of The Day

THIS perfect day has nearly passed,
These hours of sea and sun,
And yet one special joy remains
Before, at last, it's done.

We climb the sandy clifftop path,
Past cotton-grass and thrift.
Where rabbits graze beneath the gorse,
We wait the day's last gift.

In stillness, nature's masterpiece
Begins to now unfold.
The sun sinks low, the sky's afire,
And all the world turns gold.

And then it's gone, and nothing left
Where once the sun burned bright.
So now, as moonbeams guide us home,
We bid our day goodnight.

Maggie Ingall.

Ants!

THEY arrive all too soon, unexpected,
As soon as conditions are right,
When it's hot and it's sunny and blissful,
They hurry and worry – and bite!

But having said this, they're industrious,
They all work together to plan;
For a life form so small
They will each give their all,
And save a mate's life where they can.

If you don't want them inside your kitchen,
Put some sugar outside your door;
They enjoy things to eat
That taste very sweet,
So they won't give you grief any more.

Dawn Lawrence.

from the Manse Window

I Can See Clearly Now

LET me begin with a prayer:
*Lord, thank you for the gift of
sight today,
That I can open the window and
welcome in your light.
Thank you for those glorious clouds;
I look up and anticipate your coming.
And the houses nearby; thank you
for neighbours and community.
Bless these homes with your grace
and your peace.
In the distance I can see trees and
mountains; thank you for nature,
For all that inspires worship, and for
the call to adventure!
Thank you for the unseen angels
that stand guard at our door
And for the birds of the air, robins
and wagtails that land
And scurry alongside as I step to
my car;
Chirpy companions, friends you give
us for free!
Lord, open our eyes to see you at
work in your world,
And our lives today.
Help us see your smile in the
beauty and the colour,
Your reflection in human creativity
and ability,*

*And your face in the faces of those
in need.
Help us see your holiness and
grace even in the tragedies,
The perplexing, hideous atrocities of
human depravity.
Help us to look with compassion on
the multitude,
Like our Master does.
Thank you for the gift of vision
today.
Open our eyes; help us see.
Amen.*

In his 1998 song "My Father's
Eyes", veteran rock artist Eric Clapton
poignantly expressed a double tragedy
in his life.

The first was that he never knew his
father, never got to look in his eyes
and see the love of a proud dad. The
second was the tragic accidental death
of his son Conor, aged just four.

As the song struggles with the pain
of absence and loss, the singer
expresses some degree of comfort
and resolution that perhaps the child
had similar eyes to his unknown
grandfather. Perhaps, even for a short
time, Clapton had been looking
in his father's eyes without ▶

iStock.

By Rev. Andrew Watson.

▶ knowing it.

It's a beautiful song, though deeply painful, reminding us that the gift of vision yields both joy and sorrow.

We've likely all seen some wonderful things which made our hearts soar, but also some things we wish we hadn't, things which may haunt our dreams for years to come. We long to see other things but don't. Our eyes, and hearts, grow weak with yearning.

We attend the graduation ceremony of a family member, witness and share the joy as they celebrate with their friends. It's summer and the sun is shining. Having watched our young adults spend years and many late nights studying, how glad we are to see this day! We take such delight in showing others the photographs!

But we're also saddened when we see some people drink too much and behave irresponsibly. We watch the news on TV and grieve over yet more suffering: families fleeing war zones, people experiencing the most appalling cruelty. Guiltily we feel like switching channels. We could almost wish ourselves temporarily blind.

Perhaps there is a dear one we would love to see return home. Like the Lost Son's father in Jesus's parable, we would hurry down the lane to welcome them! We would move heaven and earth if we could to see family rifts healed and friends reconciled. We pray and hope, but the waiting seems to have no end.

We cannot always choose the things we witness, but how we choose to view them is crucially important. This will largely decide if the outcomes are going to be positive or negative. Challenges can become opportunities depending on our outlook.

The Dalai Lama, exiled from his homeland in Tibet since 1959, chooses to look on life positively. He has been famously quoted as saying, "Wherever you have friends that's your country, and wherever you receive love, that's your home . . . Suffering is inevitable . . . but how we respond to that suffering is our choice."

Mahatma Gandhi, affectionately referred to as the father of modern India, campaigned tirelessly at great personal cost for an independent pluralist state.

He said, "You must be the change you wish to see in the world."

We could add words from Nelson Mandela or Martin Luther King. All of these great world visionaries could have been overwhelmed with the scale of the problems facing them and given in to bitter despair. Instead they chose to see possibilities for hope and practise love and forgiveness over hatred and resentment.

From some of history's darkest times come the most inspiring and illuminating stories.

During World War II, Corrie ten Boom, the first licensed female watchmaker in the Netherlands, was imprisoned with her family members in the Nazi death camp in Ravensbruck for helping Jews escape the Holocaust. During their incarceration both her father and sister died.

Corrie survived, and after her release, despite having witnessed and suffered the most awful brutality, worked passionately to fulfil their dream to show kindness to the vulnerable, including former Dutch collaborators. Amazingly she met with and forgave some of her former prison guards.

This remarkable lady wrote, "In darkness God's truth shines most clear." Choosing to practise faith in atrocious circumstances, she discovered her heart and soul were enriched beyond imagining.

"If you look at the world you'll be distressed, if you look within you'll be depressed. But if you look at Christ you'll be at rest." When we look at Christ in the pages of the bible, what do we find?

Take the occasion when he and his disciples were exhausted and trying to get some quiet time for rest and refreshment. They rowed across the lake only to find another huge crowd waiting: people in need of healing, food, truth, forgiveness, reassurance and love.

Tired as they were, we could imagine the Master's heart sank.

Instead we see this: "He had compassion on them, because they were like sheep without a shepherd." (Mark 9 v 36.)

He welcomed and helped all who came to him. He chose to see the opportunity in the challenge, the occasion for grace and kindness in the people's burdens.

Influenced by what one writer has called our master's "gaze of love", we may look on the world with sadness but never without compassion. As we open our eyes and look around, may we know his help to see others as he does. Often needy, sometimes lost, but always precious. ∎

Nature's Calendar For *Summer*

The International Day of Friendship takes place on July 30, and is spearheaded by the UN to draw attention to how kindness and communication can help overcome all the obstacles that prevent peace around the world.

Death Valley in the United States is home to the highest ever recorded temperature on earth, reaching a sizzling 56.7 deg. C. in July 1913. And that's just the air temperature. In Furnace Creek, the ground can reach a touch under 94 deg. C.!

un-loving aubergines are
n season in August. They
nade their way to British
ables from their Asian
rigin via Spain, then
rance. Unusually, we
ept the French word
aubergine", while many
ther English-speaking
ountries use the word
eggplant", originally used to describe
particularly egg-shaped variety.

August is a good time to spot jaguars
in Brazil's "Pantanal" – its tropical
wetlands. The grass is such a vivid
shade of green at this time of the
year that the jaguars stand out. The
biodiversity here is stunning – there
are estimated to be over 1,000
species of bird alone!

ertain species of animals like
nails, bees and hedgehogs undergo
something in summer
called aestivation.
It's the opposite
of hibernation,
in a sense
– a summer
sleep. When
temperatures
soar, these
animals seek cool
places to slumber.

*Welwitschia mirabilis is a
plant found in the deserts
of Namibia. It might not
look impressive, but it
survives in some of the
harshest conditions on
earth, only technically
grows two leaves at a time
and can live for
up to 1,500
years.*

My Earrings

I'VE got some lovely earrings
That never go astray.
Well, that's not really accurate:
I can lose them twice a day!

I've lost one in the village hall –
I feared that it had gone.
The committee sent an e-mail round:
If it's yours, we'll send it on!

I lost one in my bedroom –
At least that's what I thought.
But when I looked beneath my desk,
On the carpet it had caught.

Last week I thought that one had gone
When I snoozed on the settee.
I found it on the kitchen floor
After days, returned to me!

They are two little drama masks:
The comic and the tragic.
I think the comic's winning out –
They return as if by magic!

Elizabeth Horrocks.

The Fairy Ring

THERE in the glade – a mushroom ring!
I came on it by chance;
Forget the science, I just knew
It's where the fairies dance!

In school our class all learned the facts
Of how these rings appear,
But teachers never saw the tiny
Footprints, oh, so clear!

Perhaps when starlit darkness falls
And birds no longer sing,
We might just hear the purple bells
Of foxgloves softly ring . . .

As they call forth the faerie folk
To spread their wings and fly
And come and dance the night away
Beneath the starry sky!

For in this often hate-filled world
It would be simply tragic
If there was not the smallest space
For wisps of fairy magic!

Eileen Hay.

Sports Lover

I WANT to take my ball outside
And run around, and kick it.
I asked my dad, but he won't come:
He's listening to the cricket.

My sister's locked inside her room
With rugby on her phone.
I want to practise badminton:
She shouts, "Leave me alone!"

I want to go along the street
Where there's a swimming pool.
I'm far too young to go alone
(My mother made that rule).

She's sitting in the living-room,
With tennis on TV.
"No, dear, not this afternoon,
It's Wimbledon, you see."

My family can't understand
Why I'm kicking up a fuss.
They say, "It's such a pity
You don't like sport, like us!"

Elizabeth Horrocks.

The Colours Of Autumn

AS memories of summer fade,
The signs of autumn are displayed;
Ripe hazelnuts and blackberries,
And acorns falling from the trees.

A time of plenty all around
With windfalls littering the ground,
Like apples, pears and plums galore;
A feast for animals to store.

Redundant leaves are tumbling down;
In yellows, reds and golden brown,
All blown and scattered everywhere
And soon the trees are almost bare.

But walking down a country lane,
Beside a field of golden grain,
Or purple heather on the hill
Are things that can delight us still.

The autumn show is at its best,
But – for a while – it's time to rest.
The signs are there in subtle ways:
Longer shadows, shorter days.

As we prepare for harsher times
And birds depart for warmer climes,
The winds begin to feel quite raw
With winter knocking at the door . . .

Dennis W. Turner.

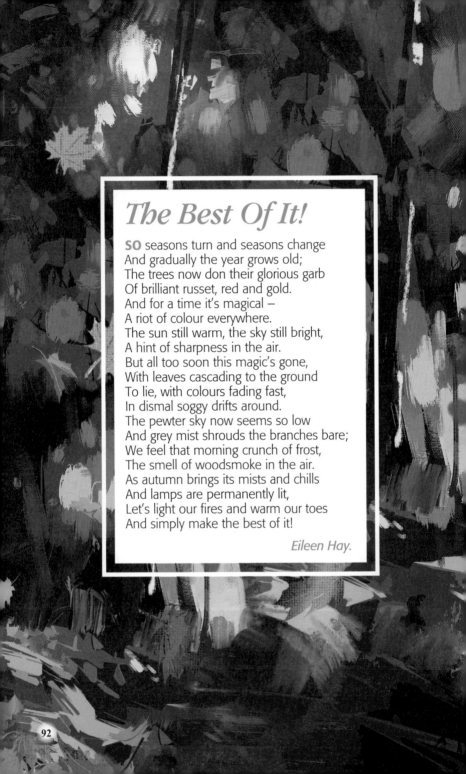

The Best Of It!

SO seasons turn and seasons change
And gradually the year grows old;
The trees now don their glorious garb
Of brilliant russet, red and gold.
And for a time it's magical –
A riot of colour everywhere.
The sun still warm, the sky still bright,
A hint of sharpness in the air.
But all too soon this magic's gone,
With leaves cascading to the ground
To lie, with colours fading fast,
In dismal soggy drifts around.
The pewter sky now seems so low
And grey mist shrouds the branches bare;
We feel that morning crunch of frost,
The smell of woodsmoke in the air.
As autumn brings its mists and chills
And lamps are permanently lit,
Let's light our fires and warm our toes
And simply make the best of it!

Eileen Hay.

Golden Days

CAN we believe the changes now?
The colours turning on the bough:
Ochre, russet and tangerine,
Gold and orange, dress the scene.
Season's music changes, too:
Snapping twigs, sounding anew,
The kick and crunch, a rustling stir –
A serenade this time of year.
And by the fender burnished bright
We embrace the mellow night;
Autumn is here for just a while,
So let us celebrate in style.

Dorothy McGregor.

Bad Hair Day!

I'VE combed it out, and fluffed it up,
Made waves where there were none;
But since the day is wild and wet,
My hair is having fun.
It refuses to stay where it's put,
Although I brush each tress;
It's determined just to irritate
And cause me lots of stress.

On wet and windy days, my hair
Sticks out in all directions
With frizzy, grizzly attitude,
That makes for imperfections.
Just why it should behave this way
Is hard to diagnose;
It might be that it frizzes so,
Since that's the way it grows.

But when the day is wet or damp,
That's when it's always worse –
When I get most frustrated,
And the reason why I curse!
So if anyone has some ideas
On the best way to proceed –
I will welcome their instructions
And be very glad, indeed!

Dawn Lawrence.

Around The World

WHEN my thoughts begin to fly,
They take me far from home,
To some exotic island
Or a desert dry as bones.

They take me over tree tops,
To the very highest hill,
Or the Austrian snow-capped mountains
Where the air is thin and chill.

They take me to the Arctic
Where the polar bears survive,
Or freezing white Antarctica,
Where penguins dip and dive.

Then the white sands of Barbados,
Where the crystal waves flow by.
Staring at horizons,
As the clear sea meets the sky.

They take me up the Eiffel Tower,
And then the Empire State,
The Pyramids of Egypt,
The Louvre or the Tate.

Over forests of Malaysia,
Where the apes screech and swing by,
Or the frozen wastes of Russia,
Where the cold winds bite and sigh.

I can float around the Dead Sea
Or watch where eagles soar,
I can trek through Tanzania,
Where the lionesses roar.

I love where dreams can take me,
Round the world and flying free,
But home is where the heart is,
And it's where I'd rather be.

Linda Brown.

from the Manse Window

Time To Give Thanks

DO you recall your parents saying to you in bygone days, "Remember to say thank you"? I certainly do! The "two magic words", as they are often referred to, are so important in many situations of life.

Thank you is one of the dominant themes of the prayers we offer to God: thanks for the gift of life; thanks for the wonder and beauty of creation; thanks for the gift of families and friendships and for the standard of living we enjoy; thanks for the good food that nourishes our bodies and for the many special gifts we have each been given, not to mention the countless luxuries we all enjoy.

When autumn leaves start to fall, the time around which the harvest of field and orchard is safely gathered in, the farming community especially says thank you for the fertile ground and for the miracle of growth year after year.

However, at all times and in all seasons, summer and winter, seedtime and harvest, saying thanks to God and to others is vitally important. On occasions thanks is rather short

lived, because with some people thankfulness can be temporary. All too soon they are caught up in their old way of life and any thankfulness they felt and expressed is gone.

Sir Winston Churchill once told the story of a sailor who one afternoon dived into the water at Plymouth Harbour to save the life of a little boy. Three days later the sailor met the boy and his mother in the street.

The sailor saw the young lad nudge his mother, whereupon she stopped the sailor and asked, "Are you the man who pulled my son out of the water?"

Anticipating an expression of gratitude from the lady, the sailor smiled, saluted and said, "Yes, ma'am, it was me."

"Thank you," the child's mother replied, "but where's his cap?"

But true heartfelt gratitude really does make a difference. Life is God's gift to each one of us, and we certainly ought to be thankful for that!

Few folks have learned and practised this truth as Paul the Apostle has.

In a letter Paul once wrote to ▶

iStock.

By Rev. Ian W.F. Hamilton.

▶ the early Christian church, he lists the basic qualities which are essential to build a new and real life – things like compassion, kindness, humbleness of mind, meekness, long-suffering, mutual forebearance, forgiving one another, and love.

At the end of the list Paul goes on to say, in no uncertain manner, "In all circumstances, give thanks, whatever happens . . . remember to say thank you."

Paul himself did his very best to live by that philosophy. Towards the end of his life he penned some other words, revealing words from his prison cell in Rome.

In thanking the church for all their gifts, he wrote, "I have learned in whatever state I am, therewith to be content."

Paul had to learn this because this kind of attitude towards life doesn't come easy to anyone. It's certainly not easy to be content and thankful in every circumstance life throws at us.

The story is told of a minister who, while on holiday at a coastal resort, decided to look up a friend – a man who had been one of his former elders. The minister's friend had retired to this holiday town some years before, but he now wasn't living at the address the minister had in his diary.

After some investigation he traced the former elder to a recently constructed block of flats which overlooked the seaside town's beautiful bay.

The man was overjoyed to meet his old minister again and cordially welcomed him to his relatively new abode. The minister immediately remarked on the wonderful flat that his friend had been recently allocated, with every mod-con imaginable.

"Yes," his friend said. "I was so grateful to get it, and just look at this view!"

Nothing strange, you may think, in that, except that the minister's friend was now blind. Yet he was content and thankful that other people could enjoy the tremendous panoramic view from the window of his flat that his loss of sight denied him.

Like this man who had been denied the gift that most have been blessed with, we must always remember to say thank you; not just for the blessings we have received, but for the blessings others have received. Thanks really does make a difference.

"Thank you" or the equivalent "Ta" is one of the first words in a child's vocabulary. However, as we mature and put away childish things, we must remember to be conscientious about what we were taught at such a young age, and as the years go by we must never take thanks for granted.

It's so easy to forget to say thank you. In times of joy, when pleasant surprises come our way, when the sun is shining and the sky is cloudless, how easy it is to simply forget to say thank you – especially to God for all his blessings and happiness. We become so caught up in the happiness that God has given us that these two magic words slip our minds.

For those of us who still count good road manners as important, I'm sure, like me, nowadays you are often quite surprised when another driver actually does acknowledge your courtesy, when you give him right of way or let him out. How easy it is to take thanks for granted, both with our fellow man and with God.

In conclusion, I must practise what I preach! It is always an esteemed privilege to contribute to this annual publication. I am grateful to be invited to write something, and to those of you who patiently and kindly read it – thank you! ■

Nature's Calendar For *Autumn*

Autumn marks the time when many animals are looking for mates. Some, like deer, fight it out in violent clashes of antlers, but the humble bat has a far more civilised approach and prefers to serenade potential partners. The songs are apparently just audible, but can be best heard with a bat detector, which converts their songs to audible frequencies.

September 24 sees Americans mark National Punctuation Day, dedicated to raising awareness of common errors. We all learn the rules at school, but unless you work with words for a living (like we do), it can be hard to remember all the idiosyncrasies of the written word.

Heather carpets the hills with colour at the end of summer. It grows short and thick, to keep it stable during strong winds. During the winter months, heather is burned by gamekeepers to ensure a supply of young shoots for animals to eat, but is managed to ensure plenty of established plants are undamaged to provide habitat.

Sicily is lovely in September – still very warm, but without the bustle of the August crowds. The sea is still pleasant enough to swim in, and – if that weren't enough – an international festival of artisan *gelato* is held around the end of the month!

White truffles are coming into season through early autumn, with truffle fairs taking place in Italy in October and November. The hilly districts of Piedmont and Tuscany are particularly popular places for fairs, with guides who will take you on your own truffle hunt!

It's not uncommon for talk to turn to Indian summers when September rolls around. The phenomenon of a late burst of dry and bright weather is actually very rare. The saying is thought to originate from Native American culture, where the continued good weather was a bonus for extending the hunting season.

Pie In The Sky

I WAS just a little apple, growing up on high,
When, suddenly, I found myself chopped up in a pie!
They sprinkled me with sugar and smothered me with cream.
And then, thank goodness, I woke up and found it was a dream!
Yet, I know we apples have a vital role to play,
And there's no way that we can hang about in trees all day.
So, to prove I mean it, and that I'm not all talk,
Just spare a thought for little me, whenever you eat pork!
Or think of all the children, playing games with ropes and skippin',
Who take a bit of sheer delight in a Cox's Orange Pippin.
And there's another aspect that makes my spirit soar,
And never fails to thrill me to my very core:
It's the fact that it's accepted, and oft said with a sigh,
That the special one you love is the "Apple of your eye"!

Brian H. Gent.

A Woodland Walk

WITH bobble hats and scarves and gloves
The grandchildren are good to go,
And off we set with eager steps
Our cheeks and noses all aglow!
The trees are at their glorious best
And we can't help but stand and stare
At golds and reds and russet browns,
Our warm breaths frosting in the air.
The day is crisply fresh and sharp
And leaves are falling all around;
The children jump to catch each one
Before it spirals to the ground!
The early autumn sky is bright
With tepid warmth still in the sun.
We meet a dog who's playing in
The leaves – he's having so much fun!
It's such a privilege to have
These woods in which we're free to roam,
But soon I hear the plaintive cry,
"We're hungry now! Can we go home?"

Eileen Hay.

Autumn Shades

ON a lovely clear night in autumn
A sunset, cerise and gold,
Ebbing in the horizon
As new mellow moments unfold.
A rook looms darkly in a barn;
An owl is in the trees,
His pince-nez eyes are watching
For movement in the leaves.
And majestic autumn moon,
Immense in the inky blue,
We can almost reach and touch you –
Burnished magic, ever new.

Dorothy McGregor.

Woodsmoke In The Air

LATE autumn, nature shutting down
With trees now stark, their branches bare,
And melancholy mists that mix
With acrid woodsmoke in the air.

The garden rests, its work now done,
The seeds and bulbs all gathered in
And labelled in the potting shed,
Awaiting new life to begin.

The days are short, the daylight dim
And people hunch against the cold,
And this is when good neighbours check
On those house-bound, sick or old.

We rarely see a glimpse of sun
With early darkness black as night.
The valiant streetlamps try to shine,
But misty halos dim their light.

The pewter pavements, slick with ice,
Mean walking with utmost care;
I long for home, to build the fire
And add my woodsmoke to the air!

Eileen Hay.

Dust Bunnies

MY house is very welcoming
To creatures great and small,
But one sort's taking over –
As you come into the hall.

You'll see them scurry out of sight
And hide under the chair.
Now come into the living-room
And meet the others there.

They romp and play throughout
   the house,
In every room they're found.
They're soft and rather hairy, and
They never make a sound.

They've lots of hiding places
But like to play a game
And peep out at my visitors
(My cleaning's put to shame).

Though easy to look after
I'd give them all away,
But they seem to like it here
And here they want to stay!

Eliza Barret.

The Clothes Hoarder

THERE'S quite a struggle going on
Behind my wardrobe door;
The clothes inside are so crammed tight
There's just no room for more.
Three layers of clothes share hangers,
Competing for a space;
Some that I scarce remember –
Some which I could not trace.

But hoarding is a habit
That's difficult to break:
Some things are sentimental –
And kept for old times' sake!
Or maybe there's another cause
That's hopeful (not too wise),
"If I wait a little longer
I might go down one size!"

I can't find things I really want –
It drives me to despair
When I have to sort out tons of clothes
To find something to wear!
So, please, if you have some ideas,
Then pass them on to me;
Or if you need to borrow some,
I'll pass them on for free!

Dawn Lawrence.

117

Autumn Days

AUTUMN mists and mellow fruits;
Apples on the grass;
Pumpkins grinning on the steps –
The days are passing fast.

Though summer's rays still light the sky
A chill is in the breeze.
The final flowers fringe the lawn
Beneath the golden trees.

Breathing in the smoky air;
Fireworks in the park.
The changing hour hastens on
That cosy winter dark.

October's hazy sunlit days,
November's chilly showers;
Each year a pleasure to enjoy
Those fleeting autumn hours.

Carla Burns.

from the Manse Window

Keeping Up Appearances

'M not really into fashion – never have been – yet I get excited when the autumn lines come into the stores.

Every week I go into town and have a coffee and a muffin before I browse around the shops.

I love to see the summer colours, yet I very rarely buy any summer clothes. A lot of the pretty dresses and tops are designed to be worn by young women and I can't say that I'm young any more! But there's something about coats and boots and woolly jumpers that really gets me interested, so I always plan to replenish part of my wardrobe in the autumn.

Once the colder weather comes we need to dress appropriately (which reminds me that I probably need to buy new waterproofs this year!)

What is true for fashion is also true for us as Christians – we need to wear appropriate "clothes" for who we are. So Paul writes to the Colossians: "Clothe yourselves with compassion, kindness, humility, gentleness, patience . . . and over all these virtues put on love" (Col 3:12b, 14).

Why? Because you are "God's chosen people, holy and dearly loved" (Col 3:12a). If you claim to be a Christian then you need to show that you are in the way you live and the sort of person you are.

Someone once wrote, "I'll believe in a redeemer when Christians can show me they're redeemed", and he had a point. It's easy to say the right things, but to engage at a deep level with God where your whole life is transformed is challenging.

It's not about pretending to be something we're not. Again Paul writes to the Ephesians: "You were taught with regard to your former way of life to put off your old self which is being corrupted by its deceitful desires, to be made new in the attitude of your minds, and to put on the new self, created to be like God in true righteousness and holiness" (Eph 4:22-24).

Who makes us new? It's God. But that's not the end of the story. There are consequences to being given this new life; we have to live it. It's a choice and it's not always easy.

The Pharisees and Scribes in

iStock.

By Rev. Susan Sarapuk.

Jesus's day got it wrong. They were trying to live in the right way, but it was all about obeying rules and regulations. When they managed to do it they could say, "I'm better than you." They wanted people to be in awe of them and what they'd attained. And because they'd worked so hard at being good they felt they'd achieved something by their own efforts. There was no humility or compassion or sense of really needing God.

Jesus condemned such self-righteousness. He commended and sought out the dregs of society because they knew they weren't good enough and that they needed God. The religious people had no hunger, no need – they thought they'd worked it out for themselves.

Transformation begins when we come to that point of acknowledging who we are and who God is. That's when he can begin his work in us. One of my favourite bible verses is Philippians 1:6 – "He who began a good work in you will carry it on to completion until the day of Christ Jesus."

It reminds me that God has promised to get me through to the end.

But that promise doesn't excuse us from working with him to become the people we are called to be. The challenge of Christian living is the Sermon on the Mount, and these verses and others of Paul's that encourage us to clothe ourselves in a particular way. Yes, God will give us the will and the ability to do good, but we have to then go out and do it, and often we will be asked to make hard choices.

We've all heard of people who are able to forgive someone who's done them a great wrong. That's not an easy thing to do. Often it's a long road of wrestling with feelings and faith.

In the end, if faith wins there's a quiet trusting that ultimately there will be justice. Forgiving releases the person who does the forgiving from bitterness. It even releases a way for God to work in the life of the person who's perpetrated the wrongdoing.

I've often wondered what Jesus meant when he said, "If you forgive the sins of others they are forgiven; if you retain them they are retained" (John 20:23).

I think it must be something along these lines. Forgiving opens pathways for God to work. If we choose to deny what we say, we believe by the way we live then the door closes to others being able to see God in and through us.

So, we clothe ourselves with compassion, kindness, humility, gentleness and patience, among other qualities. We pray that God will change our hearts and then we look for every opportunity to display those qualities.

You might not feel kind or compassionate, but what matters is the action of doing kind and compassionate things. The feelings will follow. After all, you can't hate someone you're praying for and actively helping once God starts to work in your heart.

We cannot sit back and say, "God needs to change other people" as if we've arrived. God always needs to change us.

When someone has hurt us, or gossiped about us, or received something we really wanted, we're encouraged to take the attitude of humility, to be like Jesus. See it as an opportunity to grow in grace, to put on the lovely things of Jesus. Some of our churches would be happier places if we took these things seriously.

Lightweight, flimsy yet pretty summer clothes won't do for the autumn – we need something more substantial.

And lightweight, flimsy Christianity won't do – God calls us to more substantial living, to go deeper than the surface. ∎

Nature's Calendar For *Autumn*

Hitachi Seaside Park on the Pacific coast of Japan is home to hundreds of stunning plants, including these Kochia, which turn red during October. It's also known as fireweed for a number of reasons, including that it is both one of the first plants to grow back after a fire, and that it is highly flammable in hot weather, often starting fires.

Low autumn sun and dewy mornings are a great time to see spiders' webs out and about. As strong as steel, but able to flex up to five times their length without breaking, spider silk "draglines" are remarkable. They can also withstand temperatures as low as -40 deg. C. and up to 220 deg. C.

iStock.

Separation Day is a public holiday every year on November 3 in Panama. The country spent 300 years under the rule of Peru, before becoming part of Colombia. In 1903, Panama disagreed with Colombia about the possible building of the canal by the US, and the countries went their separate ways – with the US helping Panama set up on its own.

November is a great time to visit countries that would otherwise be just too warm. Oman's reputation as a destination has been building over the last few years, with many saying it's a last chance to see hints of old Arabia without the excesses of Dubai and Abu Dhabi. But be quick: apparently the country is heading fast towards the future.

Parsnips love a crisp frost, and the end of autumn finds them at their sweetest. Roast them with a few tablespoons of balsamic vinegar and brown sugar to bring out their best.

November is rainy season in Indonesia, with the island of Bali receiving an average of 70mm for the month. By comparison, there isn't one month in the Lake District with an average rainfall that low – even the driest month drops 90mm of rain, with November offering up to 227mm!

A Little Life

IT'S just an old chair by the fireside
Where the shadows creep up the wall;
A heavy, upholstered, dusty old chair,
With wings that make it look tall.

At night when the shadows grow longer,
Out from its depths creeps a mouse
Who lives there in quiet contentment,
As close as he can to his house.

He has no great expectations,
No worries or troubles has he;
He sits there cleaning his whiskers
As meek as a small mouse can be.

It is warm in the old chimney corner,
In the place where the armchair stands tall;
It is somewhere that offers shelter
To a creature so tiny, so small.

And each hour he spends in the firelight
Is a good enough reason to stay;
Just a little more life to warm his heart,
And help him survive each day.

Dawn Lawrence.

Seasonal Reflections

SUDDENLY it is September
And the calendar can't lie,
But still sunlight, mellow, tender,
Smiles on us as time goes by.
Leaves are turning red and gold,
Seasons gradually unfold.

Children go out trick or treating,
All dressed up for Hallowe'en.
Pumpkin lanterns send a greeting,
Dancing lights in windows seen,
And every little witch or ghost
Thinks their costume stands out most!

November brings the fireworks soaring,
Showering colour on the sky;
Sparklers gleaming, rockets roaring,
Noise and light, below, on high.
Parkin and treacle toffee wait,
To mark a very special date.

A few days later, people gather
To remember those who fell,
Thoughts of grandfather, great-grandfather,
Bugles sound and memories swell.
And poppies proudly bloom on stone,
Some of them for the unknown.

Deborah Mercer.

Blackberries!

SOME children talking caused me to remember
How I gathered blackberries one September:
I gathered golden rod and thyme,
I tasted sloes – and thought of wine.
Then as the wind awoke across the weald,
I watched the thistledown race up the field;
I sat beneath a friendly tree,
Spread out my hankie; ate my tea;
Then blackberried some more, until
I had no basket left to fill.
The homeward journey seemed like miles
Across the fields, and climbing stiles;
Then reaching home – oh, what a sight!
You'd swear that I'd been in a fight!
Scratched hands, torn dress, stained arms and face;
All black and purple – what a disgrace!

Dawn Lawrence.

This Time Of Year

ICE or snow or simply rain –
Wintertime is here again,
And so, you ask, should we complain?
I think, indeed, we might!

The days are short, the nights are long,
The sun is weak, the wind is strong,
And spring is slow to come along
And put the cold to flight.

Yet should I try to change my view?
There are some things it's nice to do.
This time of year brings pleasures, too,
That make the days seem bright.

Woodland walks with icy spark,
Graceful branches, bare and stark,
Home again before it's dark,
Where all is warmth and light.

A chat with friends beside the fire,
While watching cheerful flames dance higher –
There nothing more I could desire,
And winter's sheer delight!

Maggie Ingall.

The Pond In Winter

IN summer, it will be a place
Of life pulsating from the dawn,
Of damselflies' sweet, short-lived grace,
Birds diving to feed the new born.
Glinting light and welcome shade,
Nature's bounty all displayed.

Yes, time will pass and summer come,
And wings will glisten, bright eyes gleam,
And every chirp, and call, and hum
Will hover in the air and seem
Fragile, yet enduring, too –
A world where all is bright and new.

But now, this frosty winter day,
The pond, at first, seems dead and cold.
Dark storm clouds hide each wavering ray,
Yet – look more closely, and behold:
Life is there, constant, reborn,
Through every blast and every storm.

Fish survive the winter there,
Even beneath the icy crust,
When all seems desolate and bare,
We only need to wait and trust,
And life will echo and abound
And swim, and soar, and circle round.

A skein of geese swoops overhead,
A honking chevron's fearless flight
Above the pond where they are fed
By children, where the sun is bright.
And – breaking in my reverie –
A cheeky robin chirps at me!

Deborah Mercer.

Raindrops

ON my window the raindrops come pattering down
With their comforting, chattering sound.
And I think how they came, falling out of the sky,
Where they've been, before reaching the ground.

They jumped on a sunbeam that shimmered quite close,
From the sunbeam they climbed to the sky –
Higher than ever they'd travelled before,
And no-one could see them race by.

And the winds that they met were the friendliest winds
Who took them on rapturous rides;
They crossed the great seas upon gigantic waves –
But the ships had to wait for the tides.

They came from where monkeys live in the trees.
They saw green bananas turn gold;
Where children could play every day on the sands,
And nobody ever feels cold.

I just like to think how travelled they are,
To think how their stories unfold –
They gather together; they crowd and they cling,
Together how tightly they hold.

With some drops that weigh rather more than the rest,
I watch as they slip down the pane;
And now when I see them what comes to my mind
Is how they became drops of rain.

Dawn Lawrence.

Out Of Bounds

I DO not visit Might Have Been,
That unfulfilled estate,
For it's located far away
And I'd arrive too late.

Though castles there float in the air
And dreams have all come true,
There's heartsease growing all around
And skies, of course, are blue.

Whilst landscapes are inviting
And the climate just to suit,
Flowers have no perfume
And vines can bear no fruit.

So I will stay in Here And Now
Where skies are sometimes grey.
I will not visit Might Have Been,
Lest I should wish to stay.

Tricia Sturgeon.

The Comedy Skaters

YOUNG Mrs Duck and several chums
Decided on a whim
That though the ground was hard with frost
They might just have a swim!
They waddled through the frozen grass
To reach the water's edge.
Young Freddie Frog, his eyes agog,
Was watching from a ledge.

Those stalwart ladies launched themselves
With mighty vim and vigour,
But then came "Argh!" And "Squawk!" And "Help!"
Which made bad Freddie snigger.
They slid, they twirled, they spun around,
Bills open in sheer fright!
With webbed feet paddling in the air
They made a comic sight!

They could not keep their dignity
However hard they tried.
And all this time young Freddie Frog
Just laughed until he cried.
They swooshed, they swirled, they tried to stand,
But splat! Back down they went!
At last they scrambled to the bank
And flopped, completely spent!

Poor Mrs Duck, quite traumatised,
Went home to Mr Drake –
"My dear, you won't believe," she said,
"What happened at the lake!"

Eileen Hay.

from the Manse Window

The Perfect Gift

I HAPPENED to be leafing through a newspaper recently when I was intrigued by the sight of a small headline: "Generosity Can Make The World A Happier Place".

Reading on, I discovered that it was a report of an experiment in which 50 people had each been given a small sum of money and told that they could choose to spend it either upon themselves, or upon a gift for a loved one.

The result: those who made the latter choice turned out to be the most contented with their decision. And why? Because the neurons triggered by their generous behaviour activated the ventral striatum, the part of the brain associated with happiness.

Well, I guess we all knew that, didn't we? (Oh, all right, I admit I didn't.) But even though I might not have been aware of the science behind it, I'm fairly certain that I wouldn't have needed an experiment to show me what I've long observed for myself, which is that those people who are the most inclined to be generous also seem to be the people most inclined to be cheerful.

However, what the article did do was set me thinking about all the ways in which we can be generous.

Although most of us, I'm sure, enjoy the chance to give a present, to entertain friends or to drop a donation into a collection tin, I wonder is that the only way, and is it enough?

I don't imagine I'm the only one to indulge in the occasional spot of day-dreaming about all the good causes I would help, if only I happened to come into a large fortune.

But alas, the chances of that happening to any of us are not great.

The better news is that, although the experiment described in the paper may have relied upon hard cash, it is not actually crucial to the act of being generous. The opportunities for our neurons to activate our ventral striatum are still many and varied!

So if we haven't got a bottomless purse, what else can we give?

I suppose that the first and most obvious commodity is also our most precious, and that is time. So many good causes rely upon ▶

iStock.

By Maggie Ingall.

143

▶ time donated by willing volunteers. Some offer lifts or run errands, some help in charity shops, visit patients in hospitals, help to run little museums or keep large stately houses and gardens open for the public to enjoy – the possibilities are endless.

Other people offer their expertise. One acquaintance of mine is always willing to put up shelves or paint cupboards for those in need, while another, now retired from his office job, is a whizz at helping folk to fill in complicated official forms. Others prefer to offer their energy, doing tasks such as mowing lawns or dog walking.

The great thing about this form of giving is that the rewards are so often reciprocal. The young woman who lives next door to me told me how, when she first moved into her new house, she joined a local choir dedicated to entertaining people in day clubs or residential homes.

"It was the best thing I could have done," she told me, "because it immediately introduced me to a whole lot of potential new friends, not forgetting the pleasure I get from performing. The smiles and applause we receive from our audiences more than make up for all the time we spend in rehearsal."

But what if our free time is more limited? Well, it doesn't take too long to call in and say hello to a lonely neighbour. Or even to take a moment to pick up litter on the walk to work.

One such public-spirited citizen found himself the surprised but gratified recipient of a Certificate of Thanks presented by his neighbours.

"I didn't even realise they'd noticed me doing it!" he marvelled.

What if you have no time at all, or are simply unable to commit yourself to anything right now? Well, I never forget the words of a much-loved uncle of mine.

"Generosity," he pronounced, "is a funny thing. If you can cultivate generosity of spirit, then it doesn't matter if you haven't a spare penny to give away – you can still make the world a better place."

As a child, I wasn't quite sure what he meant, but as the years have gone by I've come to understand far more clearly. Unfortunately I suspect we've all come across one or two people who are the absolute opposite of what my uncle intended: people who can't bring themselves to offer anything but hard words and disapproval.

Happily, there are far more folk who have nurtured the habit of open-heartedness, of generosity both in attitude and deed. People who are always willing to listen and to give their full attention. People who offer encouragement rather than negativity, praise rather than criticism, and who invariably make us feel more positive about ourselves. None of this costs their donors money, or even much time – but oh, the difference they make.

By now you may be wondering why such a relatively short article has prompted such long musings on the subject. Well, perhaps it's something about this time of year, for autumn itself is a kindly season, with its abundant harvests, its joyful festivals, and its rich bounty of flowers, fruit and vegetables, freely given and shared throughout the community.

And just as we start to lose the golden days to the colder and darker days of winter, we see the bright star of Christmas beginning to shine its clear and steadfast light towards us.

That is a sign to remember the greatest gift of all: the gift of love and joy and hope, all wrapped up in the shape of a newborn baby, lying in a manger. A gift to each and every one of us for now and all time.

Rejoice! ■

iStock.

Nature's Calendar For *Winter*

Naturally built for winter, wolverines do not hibernate but specialise in hunting in cold and remote locations. Their paws are wide and work like snowshoes, and their claws are excellent at keeping grip on slippery surfaces. They also roam widely in winter, too – one wolverine was discovered to have ranged over 500 miles in a little over 40 days.

December 15 sees the tea-producing nations of the world mark International Tea Day. Countries like Sri Lanka, Vietnam and Tanzania celebrate their popular and enormous industry, but it's also a chance to draw attention to the workers' conditions and other challenges the tea business faces.

146

iStock.

Roasted chestnuts have been a Christmas staple for generations. They were originally cooked in the mountainous areas of Europe, at a time of year when many grains were unavailable. Chestnuts are the only nuts with a meaningful amount of Vitamin C in them.

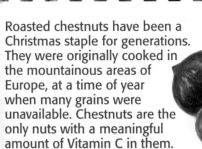

What could be more festive than Christmas in New York? From the Radio City Christmas Spectacular that's been entertaining crowds since 1933, to the Rockefeller Center tree-lighting ceremony, it's hard not to feel the festive spirit on these famous streets – especially on Fifth Avenue where the shop window displays are probably the world's finest.

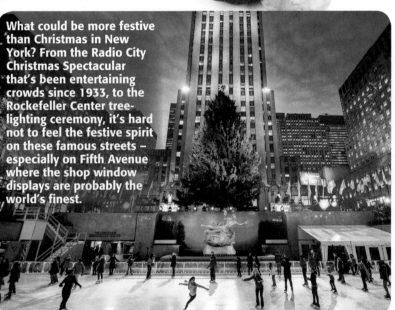

Hardy rosemary survives the winter well, although don't take too much off, as it naturally slows growth right down except in the mildest conditions. There's some evidence that the scent of rosemary improves memory, too, with a compound that can stimulate neurotransmitters.

Yakutsk has the lowest average winter temperatures of any city in the world. Think it's a bit brisk outside? Imagine daily temperatures of -39 deg. C. – that's cold enough to freeze mercury.

Seashore In Winter

'TIS a lonely place where the grey sea foam
Laps a pebbled shore, and the seagulls roam
In a grey-black sky where dull clouds blow,
Sculling white horses to and fro.

Where dark granite cliffs loom above the sand
And cormorants screech across the land,
Where in straggled heaps lies the green seaweed,
Drying out slowly where the seabirds feed.

Where the cold sea throws its foam on the shore
As crying gulls above it soar,
Where young crabs scuttle over old fish bones
And sand hoppers sleep under cold, hard stones.

Where anemones wave from a pool in the rock
And encrusted limpets cling, tightly locked.
Where on the cliff face in the sparse damp turf,
Small flowers slowly flourish in the salty earth.

Jenny Dale.

The Moon Shines Brightly

WHEN the moon shines brightly
And it's getting cold at nights,
You might like to take a stroll with me
To see some wondrous sights.
There's a little lonely wood I know
That hides behind a hill;
I go there when the village sleeps
And all the air is still.

We'll sit around a cheerful fire
Of crackling fir tree cones,
And wait – all wrapped up tightly –
As we perch on mossy stones;
For that's when all the forest folk
Come out to hunt and play:
Hedgehogs, rabbits, badgers, mice,
Each one might pass our way.

You mustn't make the slightest sound;
You mustn't sneeze or cough,
Or otherwise you'll startle them
And they'll all scamper off.
We can't sit still too long, of course,
In case a cold wind blows.
Just think of all those chilblains
On our fingers and our toes!

Dawn Lawrence.

Time Flies

ONE thing's sure, you'll hear folk saying,
Didn't time fly past this year?
As the shops are all displaying
Harbingers of Christmas cheer,
Lights and baubles for the tree,
And thousands of cards to see.

Winter brings us children's faces,
Bright and flushed on Christmas Eve.
Presents stashed in hidden places,
And, yes, we still believe
That hope and peace can come to pass
In silent prayers at midnight mass.

And, of course, we know that yearly
Resolutions will be made,
Made in earnest, made sincerely,
Although most of them will fade!
But January, crisp and new,
Makes us think they could come true!

Before long our thoughts are turning
To flowers, chocolate and wine,
Young or old, we can't help yearning
For a faithful Valentine,
And hoping that love is there
In the February air!

And so we're back at the beginning,
With the earlier morning light,
Last snow melting, last frost thinning,
Shoots poke through the winter white.
Winter's ending, spring's soon here –
This is the dawning of the year!

Deborah Mercer.

The Mind's Eye

ONCE upon a time ago,
When fairy tales were true,
And make-believe was in the air,
And winged dragons flew.
When just around each corner lay
Adventure and delight,
Hours were spun from rainbows
And dreams fit snuggly tight.
And life stretched all around us
As far as eye could see,
With wonders there a-beckoning
And buttered toast for tea.

But Time, alas, decrees that myth
And magic have to go.
For fantasy is only real
When we are sure 'tis so.

Tricia Sturgeon.

Monster Attraction

WAY back in old cretaceous times,
At Blackpool by the sea,
A teenage pterodactyl went
Upon a spending spree.

He rode the giant Ferris wheel
And came down quite contented.
(Nobody thought to tell him that
It had not been invented!)

He went on all the mammoth rides
And never once showed fear,
And as his money dwindled he
Went strolling on the pier.

He played the pinballs, fruit machines
And all the other things;
He even had his fortune told
By readings of his wings!

He soon had just one penny left
And with a mighty roar
He dropped the coin into the slot
Of "Match The Dinosaur".

Dennis W. Turner.

Higgledy Piggledy Rooftops

HIGH above the city and the traffic's roar and drone,
Higgledy piggledy rooftops speak a language of their own.
While far beneath the domes and spires, people rush on by,
The rooftops stand serene and still, pointing to the sky.

I'm enchanted by their beauty in sunset's glorious flame,
Each one a unique design – no two are the same.
I picture those they've sheltered throughout the passing years:
Folk in search of warmth and hope, perhaps, in joy or tears.

May we, like the rooftops, in the clamour the world brings,
Stand serene and still and point the way to higher things.
Let each life be a shelter, offering to those in need
A sanctuary of comfort; a kindly word or deed.

As far above the city and its ceaseless roar and drone,
The higgledy piggledy rooftops speak a language of their own.
May we, though we're different, no two of us the same,
Convey those words of love to set every heart aflame.

Marian Cleworth.

The Holly Tree

I BRAVED the woods although the snow
Lay thickly on the ground,
And as I walked, huge feathery flakes
Fell gently all around.

The silence was profound and deep,
Sounds muffled by the snow,
And light and white together gave
A strangely peaceful glow.

I pushed aside a snowy branch
And there in front of me:
The only colour in the woods –
A perfect holly tree!

The glossy leaves shone deepest green;
Its berries vibrant red.
I stood and gazed in sheer delight,
Snow swirling round my head.

And then, just like a Christmas card,
A robin fluttered down.
His red breast fluffed against the cold
His feathers richest brown.

I knew that with the changing light
We neared the close of day,
And as I turned and headed home
The robin flew away.

Eileen Hay.

Little Things Matter

'VE had some mixed reactions when I've told people this, so stand by . . . I work part-time in the stockroom of a well-known retail chain.

In the run-up to Christmas 2014 I was between parishes and our local store was hiring temporary staff and I thought, why not? My application was successful, and when the contract was up in January, the management invited me to stay on. There I've been ever since, one or two shifts a week.

People do ask how it works out with now being the minister of two parishes, but with a lot of respect, understanding and flexibility on all sides it actually balances out pretty well. While some may think it not quite the thing for a member of the clergy, I've found it has given me considerable "street cred" with others.

One parishioner said, "There's no shame in it. I worked somewhere like that all my life."

My eldest son, who drives articulated lorries, was more blunt, saying, "Congratulations, Dad, you've got a real job at last!"

Personally, while I will always remain heart and soul, first and foremost a minister of Jesus Christ, committed to sharing his Gospel and building his church, I love it! Clergy deal with ultimate life and death matters such as births, weddings and funerals, not to mention faith and learning together from the Bible how to live and thrive in a positive relationship with our maker.

Nevertheless we can sometimes be guilty of existing in a closeted, slightly unreal bubble.

I hope my hours in the stockroom give me perspective on what life is like on a Monday morning for people who listen to my sermons on a Sunday. I pray it helps close the perceived gap between religion and everything else, because all of life is connected.

So do I wear a uniform? Of course, and a headset with earpiece and microphone by which I'm linked in to a highly sophisticated computer system. A robotic voice gives me the code for each location, tells me which item to pick and where to take it. It could be anything from a kettle to a trampoline, a toothbrush to ▶

iStock.

By Rev. Andrew Watson.

▶ a 55-inch widescreen TV.

Sometimes you have to say aloud characters like "bravo" or "delta" to confirm something. The machine doesn't always pick it up correctly first time, so you might have to repeat "whisky" loudly several times. Even though you know it's a robot, you might feel like getting exasperated and saying, "I said 'alpha' not 'golf', you stupid thing!" It remains impassive and repeats the instruction in flat monotone.

At the start I used to hear that voice in my dreams. My wife says one night in bed I was trying to take her to Collection Point Alpha.

And then there's the walking. You quickly lose count of the number of times it sends you to the upper stockroom to send items down the conveyor belt. I wear a step tracker and usually have my 10,000-step daily target done by lunchtime. I feel like a greyhound, albeit a fairly tired one by home time.

So why do I love it so much? Firstly it gives me an opportunity to serve the public. I love having multiple occasions to be pleasant and helpful to people in a simple, non-controversial way. Our name badges carry the message *Here To Help* and that's a pretty good attitude to life in my book.

Handing the customer their purchase with a smile and a quick chat, maybe helping people to their car with a heavier item, is a privilege. The customer may be going home to an empty house, or a situation of friction or abuse. We may be the only people to speak a kind word to them today. I for one will not miss that opportunity.

Our Lord was constantly kind to people. Welcoming and compassionate, He teaches his followers to do likewise, treating others as we would like to be treated ourselves. The apostle Paul in his letter to Colossians 3 urges us to clothe ourselves "with compassion, kindness, humility, gentleness and patience".

St Francis is credited with the wise teaching, "Preach the Gospel. Use words if necessary." In addition to my weekly pulpit ministry, I am so glad to be able each week to share the Gospel without preaching by serving strangers with joy and kindness.

Another pleasure comes from being accepted as one of the team. We have various backgrounds, beliefs and opinions about things, but instore we are colleagues and friends.

You need a hand with that barbecue or patio set? You've got it. Stuck with something on the computer? There's always someone not far away who'll help you out. We're in this together, and when the rush is on and everyone is doing their bit and supporting each other it's just brilliant.

Sometimes there will be a gift and card to sign for someone who's getting married or has had a baby, or perhaps it may be a sympathy card. Sometimes it extends informally outside business hours, visiting a colleague who's been off sick or meeting someone for coffee who's going through a rough patch.

Again, it's a privilege to share not just the work but life. It's not always easy. We have our moments, but the teamwork reminds me of Bible passages like Psalm 133, which promises blessings where people live and work together in harmony.

Finally, I like being aware that my little contribution is part of something much bigger. As I deliver that microwave to the Collection Point, I'm part of a huge operation that affects thousands of people. Little things – and little people – matter.

The couple in the stable on a busy night in Bethlehem didn't seem that significant, yet they were part of something global and eternal. Faithfully, wonderingly obeying the angels' instructions, they had only hints of something bigger.

The bigger picture was that God was sending his son to bring grace, rescue and life to the world, every nation, every person who believes.

Glad as I am to be a small part of a retail operation, I'm even more thrilled to be part of God's plan in Christ. ∎

Nature's Calendar For *Winter*

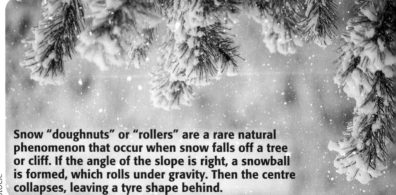

Hummingbirds enter a state of "torpor" on cold nights, when their metabolism slows down and they quite often hang upside-down. It takes a hummingbird around 20 minutes to wake up from this deep sleep, when they vibrate their wings to bring warmth back into the body.

Snow "doughnuts" or "rollers" are a rare natural phenomenon that occur when snow falls off a tree or cliff. If the angle of the slope is right, a snowball is formed, which rolls under gravity. Then the centre collapses, leaving a tyre shape behind.

iStock.

Bees won't fly if it's too cold, but in milder winters they'll be grateful for any winter-flowering plants you have around. Consider planting the lovely evergreen Mahonia, a tough plant with stunning yellow flowers that can thrive even in temperatures as low as -15 deg. C.

If you're looking for some winter sun, January is a great month to head for Central America. Countries like Costa Rica and Nicaragua offer everything from rainforest to volcanoes to sun-kissed beaches. Tiny Belize is worth exploring, too, an English-speaking former British colony that gained its independence in 1981.

Seville oranges, the classic marmalade orange, are a winter staple with a short season. They were globes of sunshine in the winters of Victorian Britain, and are especially good for marmalade thanks to their high pectin content. It helps the marmalade set, and is also one of the reasons they make excellent candied peel.

The Welsh saint of lovers Dwynwen, is celebrated on January 25 with St Dwynwen's Day. The story (in short) goes that after experiencing unrequited love Dwynwen devoted herself to the service of God in exchange for the true love of others being fulfilled in the future.

Christmas In Your Hearts

CHRISTMAS brings us many things
With laughter, love and tears,
A wealth of happy memories
All gathered through the years.
A time for reaching out once more,
A time to seek and find,
A time for sharing hope and joy,
Goodwill to all mankind.

Christmas brings us cards and thoughts
From people far away.
To know we are remembered still
Can cheer a winter day.
The songs and carols fill the air,
The streets are filled with light.
Can we recapture once again
The thrill of Christmas night?

Whatever Christmas means to you
May friendship play a part,
As through the days which lie ahead
Keep Christmas in your heart!

Iris Hesselden.

Memories

DECEMBER'S here, and so the date
Means it's time to decorate.
To deck the halls, as the song says,
Prepare the house for festive days.
And I've seen tips in magazines
For setting tasteful festive scenes.

So to the attic I repair
And see what I find waiting there.
And there I see not grace and style,
But a trusty clutter pile.
All the things that are still here
That I said I'd throw out last year.

Those baubles are tatty, it's true
(And weren't that chic when they were new!);
That silver bell is still lop-sided,
And by experts it would be derided;
The fairy lights are in a tangle,
The tree at a precarious angle.

But no, I can't get rid of these!
They are too full of memories!
The Christmas clutter seems to wait
To be dusted, be put straight,
And brought out – old friends, trusted, dear –
I'll have a think . . . Maybe next year!

Deborah Mercer.

Winter Sunset

MY footsteps quickened near the gate,
My uppermost desire
Being just to thaw my hands and feet
Before a blazing fire!
The rooftop was a silhouette
Against the glowing sky;
The frozen birdbath looked like fire
With colours from on high.
Some rooks were ravaging the thatch –
For once I did not care.
I slipped and slid along the path,
Breath frosting in the air.
The garden looked quite magical
Ablaze with red and gold.
No artist, should he paint the scene,
Would ever be so bold!
But now the sun was sinking fast,
The trees turned black and stark.
The birdbath's icy fire went out
And all the world was dark.

Eileen Hay.

"Friends are the family you choose."
– *Jess C. Scott*